How Are Living Things Connected to Their Ecosystem?

Houghton Mifflin Harcourt.

PHOTOGRAPHY CREDITS: COVER ©Diane McAllister/naturepl.com; 3 (tr) ©Victoria Martin/Shutterstock; 4 (b) ©Diane McAllister/naturepl.com; 6 (tr) ©hagit berkovich/Shutterstock; 7 (b) ©Digital Vision/Getty Images; 9 (tc) ©Daniel Dempster Photography/Alamy Images; 9 (tr) ©Victoria Martin/Shutterstock; 9 (tl) ©Dominique Landau/Shutterstock; 11 (b) ©Corbis; 12 (b) ©Jeremy Woodhouse/Photodisc/Getty Images; 13 (bc) ©PhotoLink/Photodisc/Getty Images; 13 (l) ©Image Source/Superstock; 13 (tl) Photos.com/Jupiterimages/Getty Images; 13 (tr) Photodisc/Getty Images; 14 (b) ©Comstock Royalty Free; 15 (tr) ©Joe Petersburger/National Geographic/Getty Images; 16 (tr) ©Francois Gohier/Science Source/Photo Researchers, Inc.; 17 (b) ©Jupiterimages/Getty Images

ISBN: 978-0-544-07288-6

15 0710 18

4500707313   B C D E F G

Be an Active Reader!

 Look at these words.

habitat	community	decomposer
environment	food chain	photosynthesis
ecosystem	producer	drought
population	consumer	

 Look for answers to these questions.

What makes up an environment?

How are living things organized in an ecosystem?

What different ecosystems can you find?

What is a food chain?

What are roles in a food chain?

How does energy flow in a food chain?

What happens to a food chain if a part is lost?

Do environmental changes affect ecosystems?

What makes up an environment?

Look at the great blue heron wading in the water. It has things to eat and places that provide shelter. In the heron's habitat, it finds everything it needs to survive. A habitat is the space where a plant or animal lives.

What surrounds the heron? There are plants, soil, water, air, and other animals. All of these are parts of the heron's environment. An environment is all the living and nonliving things that surround and affect an organism.

The great blue heron is a wading bird that catches its food in water.

How are living things organized in an ecosystem?

The great blue heron lives in a swamp with other organisms. All of the organisms interact with their environment. They breathe the air. They drink the water. An ecosystem is a group of organisms and the environment in which they live. Ecosystems can be divided into populations and communities.

The great blue heron is not the only bird of its kind in the swamp. There are other great blue herons living there. Together, all are called the great blue heron population. A population is all of one kind of organism living in the same ecosystem.

These great blue herons are part of a larger population.

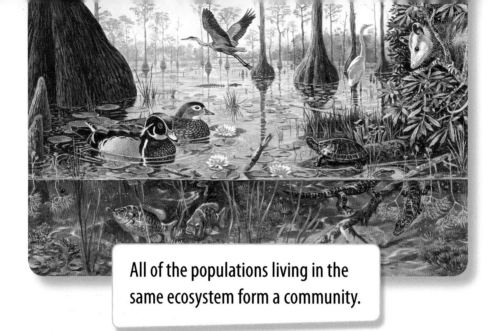

All of the populations living in the same ecosystem form a community.

The swamp ecosystem contains many other populations. For example, a population of painted turtles lives there. So does a population of water lilies. All of the populations that live and interact in an area are called a community.

You can think of an ecosystem as a community and the nonliving parts of their environment. The nonliving parts are just as important as the living ones. Without the nonliving parts, life would not be possible. For example, the swamp ecosystem could not exist without water. All of the living things depend on it.

What different ecosystems can you find?

A swamp is one kind of wetland ecosystem. Wetlands are areas of land that are covered by water much of the time. Many animals make their home in wetlands.

How is a desert different from a wetland? It is dry. Some deserts receive only about 1.5 centimeters (0.6 inches) of rain in a year. Many deserts are also hot. Deserts have plants and animals that do well in a dry climate. In a desert ecosystem, you might find cactus plants and animals such as mice, rattlesnakes, foxes, and owls.

Fennec foxes have fur on their paws to help them walk on hot desert sand.

Unlike a desert, a tropical rain forest has a wet climate with dense plant life. In a tropical rain forest ecosystem, you might find toucans and jaguars.

A temperate forest ecosystem has warm summers and cold winters. There you find animals such as squirrels and bears.

Earth also has water ecosystems. In the ocean, you can find whales, fish, and shellfish. In a river, you might see otters, fish, and turtles.

Animals have adaptations that help them survive in their ecosystems. For example, sea anemones are harmful to many kinds of fish, but not to clownfish. So, clownfish use the sea anemones to escape from other fish.

Clownfish stay safe by going where other fish don't dare to follow.

What is a food chain?

All the organisms in an ecosystem need food. Some of them, such as plants, can make their own. Other living things depend on other organisms for food. Some animals eat plants. Other animals eat other animals. Some animals eat both plants and animals.

A food chain is a series of organisms that depend on one another for food. For example, a temperate forest ecosystem has plants that make seeds. Mice eat the seeds. Hawks eat the mice.

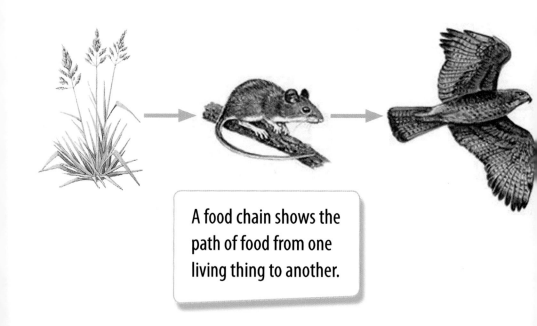

A food chain shows the path of food from one living thing to another.

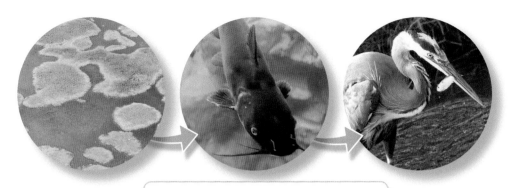

The algae, the catfish, and the heron form a food chain in the swamp ecosystem.

The great blue heron eats many kinds of things. Let's look at one great blue heron food chain. It starts with algae, tiny living things that can make their own food. They live in water. The algae are eaten by a fish called a channel catfish. The great blue heron eats the catfish.

The catfish depends on the algae for food. The great blue heron eats the catfish, but also depends on the algae for food. The algae are the first living things in the food chain.

What are roles in a food chain?

Every food chain starts with a producer. A producer is a living thing, such as algae or a plant, that makes its own food. Producers can be tiny, like algae, or large, like a tree.

What happens next? An animal eats the producer for food. Such an animal is called a consumer. A mouse is a consumer. It eats grass and seeds. Consumers that eat only plants are called herbivores.

Not all consumers eat plants. Some consumers eat other animals. Hawks eat mice. Consumers that eat only other animals are called carnivores. Consumers that eat both plants and animals are called omnivores.

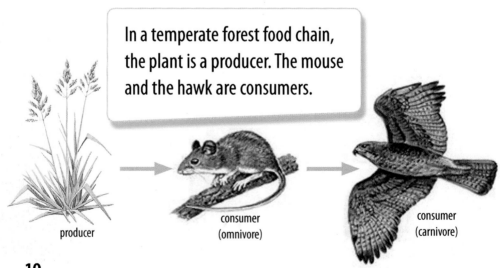

In a temperate forest food chain, the plant is a producer. The mouse and the hawk are consumers.

producer

consumer
(omnivore)

consumer
(carnivore)

Which roles do the organisms in the great blue heron food chain play? The algae are producers. The catfish and great blue heron are consumers.

Not all plants and animals get eaten. Plant leaves may fall on the ground, and an animal may grow old and die. What happens to the remains? A decomposer is a kind of consumer. Decomposers break down dead organisms and wastes into nutrients that become part of the soil.

What is this giraffe's role in its food chain? It is a consumer that eats plants.

How does energy flow in a food chain?

How do you get energy? You get it from food. The living things in a food chain get their energy from food as well.

Producers, such as plants, make their own food through a process called photosynthesis. Producers use energy from the sun. They turn carbon dioxide gas from the air and water from the ground into sugars. The sugars are the food. The producers use some of the food to grow and store the rest.

These sunflowers will store energy from the sun in their seeds.

What happens to the energy in a producer? When a consumer eats the producer, the energy moves to the animal. In the great blue heron food chain, energy from the algae moves to the catfish. The catfish uses some of the energy and stores the rest in its body. When the heron eats the catfish, the energy stored in the catfish moves to the heron. This is how energy from the sun flows from one living thing to another in a food chain.

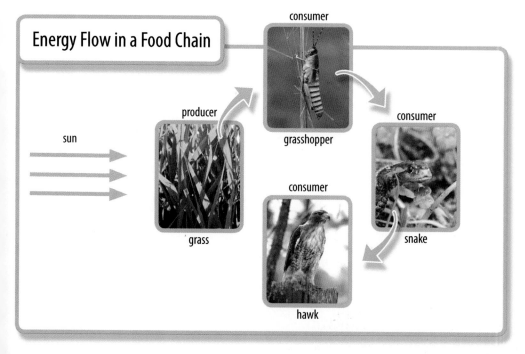

Energy Flow in a Food Chain

sun

producer
grass

consumer
grasshopper

consumer
snake

consumer
hawk

What happens to a food chain if a part is lost?

Every living thing in a food chain has a specific role. Except for the producers, each living thing consumes what is just below it. What do you think would happen if one of the living things were removed?

To think about this, imagine a field in a temperate forest ecosystem. The field has many flowering plants. Bees live off the nectar from the flowers. Other animals, such as birds and spiders, eat bees.

If the plants disappeared, the bees would not have food. Without bees, there would be less food for the spiders and birds.

Bees must move somewhere else when they lose their food source. Those who do not move cannot survive.

Now think about the heron food chain. What would happen if the algae died? The catfish might not have enough food. Some of the catfish might die. Because there would be fewer catfish, the herons would have less to eat. Some of them might die. Others might go somewhere else to find food.

This bird called a bee-eater might not survive without bees to eat.

Every living thing in a food chain depends on all the ones below it. Every part of a food chain is also important to the health of an ecosystem. Think about the flowering plants in the field. If all the flowering plants die, other animals in the forest ecosystem are affected. Rabbits that feed on the plants would not have enough to eat. Animals that feed on the rabbits would not have enough to eat, either.

Do environmental changes affect ecosystems?

You have learned how changes in populations can affect an ecosystem. What about changes in an environment?

Changes in an environment affect living things in different ways. Some living things have body parts or behaviors that help them survive changes to their environments. Other living things leave or even die.

Brittle-bush plants have adapted in a way that helps them survive dry periods. They can store water.

One environmental change is a drought. A drought is a long period of time with very little rain. Without water, animals and plants can die. Even if the animals can find water, having fewer plants means less food for them.

Another change to an environment is a flood. A flood happens when a large amount of water covers a normally dry area. When a flood occurs, plants are covered with water. Plants cannot move to dry land. Some plants die when they are covered by water. Many animals must go somewhere else to find dry land.

Erosion can also change an environment. Erosion is the process of moving weathered rock and soil from one place to another. Think of a field with few plants to keep the soil in place. The wind blows across the field, carrying away soil. When soil is removed, there is less for plants to grow in.

During a drought, elephants may travel to a new area to find water.

Make a Model

With an adult, visit a nearby natural environment, such as a field, forest, beach, or even your backyard. Notice what animals and plants live there. Try to figure out what roles they play in their ecosystem. Then make a poster with drawings of the environment, the plants, and the animals you observed. Show how the plants and animals live.

Compare and Contrast Ecosystems

Think of a change in the animals, plants, or environment that you described in your poster. Think about how the change could affect the ecosystem, and describe how it would be different from before. How could someone prevent such a change?

Glossary

community [kuh•MYOO•ni•tee] All the populations of organisms that live and interact in an area.

consumer [kuhn•SOOM•er] A living thing that cannot make its own food and must eat other living things.

decomposer [dee•kuhm•POHZ•er] A living thing that gets energy by breaking down dead organisms and animal wastes.

drought [DROUT] A long period of time with very little rain.

ecosystem [EE•koh•sis•tuhm] a community of organisms and the physical environment in which they live.

environment [en•VY•ruhn•muhnt] All the living and nonliving things that surround and affect an organism.

Glossary

food chain [FOOD CHAYN] A series of organisms that depend on one another for food.

habitat [HAB·i·tat] The place where an organism lives and can find everything it needs to survive.

photosynthesis [foh·toh·SIN·thuh·sis] The process in which plants use energy from the sun to change carbon dioxide and water into sugar and oxygen.

population [pahp·yuh·LAY·shuhn] All the organisms of the same kind that live together in an ecosystem.

producer [pruh·DOOS·er] A living thing, such as a plant, that can make its own food.